SRA

Open Court Reading

S0-BZT-956

Skills Practice

Grade 2

Mc Graw Hill Education

Bothell, WA • Chicago, IL • Columbus, OH • New York, NY

MHEonline.com

Copyright © 2015 McGraw-Hill Education

All rights reserved. No part of this publication may be
reproduced or distributed in any form or by any means,
or stored in a database or retrieval system, without the
prior written consent of McGraw-Hill Education,
including, but not limited to, network storage or
transmission, or broadcast for distance learning.

Send all inquiries to:
McGraw-Hill Education
8787 Orion Place
Columbus, OH 43240

ISBN: 978-0-07-669050-3
MHID: 0-07-669050-4

Printed in the United States of America

8 9 10 LHS 21 20

Table of Contents

/ch/ spelled *ch*, /th/ spelled *th*, and /sh/ spelled *sh*

FOCUS The letters in a consonant digraph combine to make one new sound. Some examples of consonant digraphs are /ch/ spelled *ch*, /th/ spelled *th*, and /sh/ spelled *sh*.

PRACTICE Sort the words below.
Write each word under the correct heading.

rash	thump	chap	pinch	shot
fish	with	chat	thorn	

/ch/	/th/	/sh/
1. _____	4. _____	7. _____
2. _____	5. _____	8. _____
3. _____	6. _____	9. _____

APPLY Choose a word from the box below to complete each sentence. Write the word on the line.

trash	chest	ship	thud	inch	moth	shed

10. A _____ docked in the harbor.

11. The _____ flaps its wings.

12. Sheldon fell to the floor with a _____.

13. Put all _____ in the black bin.

14. Samantha pinned a ribbon on her _____.

15. The pants are one _____ too short.

16. Our tools are in the _____.

Circle the word with /ch/ spelled *ch*, /th/ spelled *th*, or /sh/ spelled *sh*. Write the word on the line.

17. Mindy is a tennis champ. _____

18. The snow melted to slush. _____

19. Pack a lunch for the trip. _____

20. Ken will go with Skip. _____

Phonics • *Skills Practice*

/w/ spelled w*h*_ and /ar/ spelled *ar*

FOCUS
- The /w/ sound can be spelled *wh*_. A vowel always follows *wh* in this spelling of /w/.
- When the letter *r* follows a vowel, it often changes the vowel sound. When *r* follows the letter *a*, it usually makes the /ar/ sound.

PRACTICE Write the word from the box that best completes each sentence.

market	scarf	whip	when	dark	which

1. Grab a hat and a ___scarf___ before you go outside.

2. To ___which___ park should we go?

3. Come home before it gets ___dark___.

4. Use a mixer to ___whip___ the batter.

5. Get up ___when___ the alarm rings.

6. Carla got apples at the farmers' ___market___.

APPLY Use the letters in parentheses to make a word with /w/ spelled *wh_*.

7. (r, e, e) _____

8. (a, m) _____

9. (f, i, f) _____

10. (t, a) _____

Use the letters in parentheses to make a word with /ar/ spelled *ar*.

11. (d, t) _____

12. (p, s, k) _____

13. (g, d, n, e) _____

14. (h, c, m) _____

15. (n, b) _____

16. (s, p, h) _____

17. (d, h) _____

18. (y, n) _____

19. (s, t, t) _____

20. (a, r, d) _____

Closed Syllables

> **FOCUS**
> - A closed syllable occurs when a vowel spelling is followed by a consonant spelling. The vowel sound is usually short.
> - If a word has two consonant spellings in the middle, you usually divide the word between the two consonants.

PRACTICE Look at how the syllables are divided in the words below. Circle the correct way to divide each word.

1. pep/per   pe/pper

2. pic/nic   pi/cnic

3. exp/and   ex/pand

4. hic/cup   hicc/up

5. shelt/er   shel/ter

6. tu/nnel   tun/nel

7. ta/blet   tab/let

8. cob/web   co/bweb

9. bask/et   bas/ket

APPLY Divide each word into syllables.

10. mantel _____

11. rabbit _____

12. laptop _____

13. classic _____

14. temper _____

15. slipper _____

Use the above words to write five different sentences.

16. _____

_____

17. _____

_____

18. _____

_____

19. _____

_____

20. _____

_____

Phonics • *Skills Practice*

/j/ spelled ■*dge*, /k/ spelled ■*ck*, and /ch/ spelled ■*tch*

FOCUS
- The /j/ sound can be spelled ■*dge*. A short-vowel sound comes before this spelling.
- The /k/ sound can be spelled ■*ck*. A short-vowel sound comes before this spelling.
- The /ch/ sound can be spelled ■*tch*. A short-vowel sound comes before this spelling.

PRACTICE Circle the spelling for /j/, /k/, or /ch/. Then write the short-vowel spelling for each word.

1. patch _____

2. crack _____

3. tickle _____

4. ridge _____

5. batch _____

6. pledge _____

APPLY Read the words in the box. Write *dge, ck,* or *tch* in each space to spell one of the words.

| nudge | locker | stretch | pitcher | track | bridge |

7. stre_____

8. lo_____er

9. bri_____

10. pi_____er

11. nu_____

12. tra_____

Use a word from above to complete each sentence.

13. The pups _____ and sniff each other.

14. The _____ is full of milk.

15. Put your jacket in the _____.

16. Fast cars zip around the _____.

17. We bend and _____ before we run.

18. A _____ spans the big river.

Inflectional Endings -s and -es

> **FOCUS** Plural words show that there is more than one.
> Adding -s or -es to a noun makes it a regular plural.

PRACTICE Read each singular noun.
Then circle its plural form.

1. brush   brushs   brushes

2. box   boxs   boxes

3. wish   wishs   wishes

4. path   paths   pathes

5. class   classs   classes

6. chart   charts   chartes

7. champ   champs   champes

8. suffix   suffixs   suffixes

APPLY • Read each singular noun in the box.
Then write the plural form of the noun under
the correct heading.

| fox | shark | branch | hill |

-s   **-es**

9. _____   11. _____

10. _____   12. _____

Write a sentence using each plural word from above.

13. _____

_____

14. _____

_____

15. _____

_____

16. _____

_____

Inflectional Ending -ed

FOCUS • The inflectional ending -ed can be added to a base word. The meaning of the word is not changed. Only the form and function of the word changes.

• The -ed ending is used with the past tense form of a verb. It lets you know something has already happened.

PRACTICE Add -ed to each word. Write the new word on the line.

1. dodge _____

2. blossom _____

3. stretch _____

4. plan _____

5. instruct _____

6. shrug _____

APPLY Circle the correct spelling for each word. Write the correct spelling on the line.

7. tricked   trickd   _____

8. claped   clapped   _____

9. pledged   pledgeed   _____

10. expanded   expandd   _____

11. patched   patchd   _____

Use a word from above to complete each sentence.

12. Stan _____ that he would do the dishes.

13. Erin _____ her ripped jacket.

14. Martha _____ us and hid in the closet.

15. We _____ for the winners of the tennis match.

16. The balloon _____ with air.

/ng/ spelled ■ng, /nk/ spelled ■nk, Inflectional Ending -ing

FOCUS
- /ng/ is a consonant sound that is spelled ■ng.
- /nk/ is a consonant sound that is spelled ■nk.
- The ending -ing lets you know something is happening now. This ending has the /ng/ sound.

PRACTICE Sort the words below.
Write each word under the correct heading.

| rang | hung | honk | shrunk | tank | king |

/ng/

1. _____

2. _____

3. _____

/nk/

4. _____

5. _____

6. _____

APPLY Add *-ing* to the following words. Write each new word on the line.

7. drink _____

8. strum _____

9. nudge _____

10. jog _____

11. blend _____

12. swing _____

Write a word from the box that rhymes with each word below.

crank	chunk	banging	long	winking	link

13. stink _____

14. clanging _____

15. song _____

16. blank _____

17. dunk _____

18. thinking _____

Phonics • *Skills Practice*

Schwa; /əl/ spelled *el, le, al, il*

FOCUS
- The schwa sound is a vowel sound that is not stressed. The symbol for schwa is ə.
- The letters *el, le, al,* and *il* are often found at the end of words. These letter combinations make the /əl/ sound.

PRACTICE Write each word and divide it into syllables.

1. gargle _____

2. panel _____

3. metal _____

4. freckle _____

5. anvil _____

6. shrivel _____

7. shuffle _____

8. fossil _____

9. rascal _____

10. stencil _____

APPLY **Choose a word from the box below to complete each sentence. Write the word on the line.**

puddle	model	rental	gravel	tranquil

11. There are lots of nice _____ properties on this street.

12. The water was _____ before the storm started.

13. The teacher will _____ how to read fluently.

14. There was a _____ in our yard after the storm.

15. The parking lot is covered with _____.

Circle the word with the /əl/ sound. Then write the word on the line.

16. Ann's rings sparkle. _____

17. This novel is 350 pages long. _____

18. Dad makes a great lentil soup. _____

19. Apple tart is the best! _____

20. The tiger is my favorite animal. _____

Phonics • _**Skills Practice**_

/er/ spelled *er, ir, ur, ear*

> **FOCUS**
> - When *r* follows the letters *e*, *i*, *u*, or *a*, it usually makes the /er/ sound.
> - The /er/ sound can also be spelled *ear*.

PRACTICE Sort the words under the correct heading.

| slurp | heard | shirt | verb | girl | buzzer | turnip | earn |

/er/ spelled *er*

1. _____

2. _____

/er/ spelled *ir*

3. _____

4. _____

/er/ spelled *ur*

5. _____

6. _____

/er/ spelled *ear*

7. _____

8. _____

APPLY Write *er*, *ir*, *ur*, or *ear* to complete each word.

9. p_____ple

10. wh_____l

11. p_____mit

12. k_____nel

13. s_____ch

14. b_____st

Circle the word or words with /er/. Write each word on the line.

15. Jess is turning seven!

_____

16. Cam lost his sister's ring.

_____

17. Stir the pot to mix in the milk.

_____

18. Bill can earn eight dollars cutting grass.

_____

/or/ spelled *or, ore*

> **FOCUS** /or/ is a special vowel sound that can be spelled *or* and *ore*.

PRACTICE Replace the underlined letter or letters to make a word with the *ore* spelling.

1. bor<u>n</u> + e = _____

2. stor<u>m</u> + e = _____

3. por<u>t</u> + e = _____

4. tor<u>ch</u> + e = _____

5. cor<u>k</u> + e = _____

Replace the letter *e* with the new letter or letters to make a word with the *or* spelling.

6. bor<u>e</u> + der = _____

7. stor<u>e</u> + y = _____

8. por<u>e</u> + tal = _____

9. tor<u>e</u> + n = _____

10. cor<u>e</u> + n = _____

APPLY Choose a word from the box below to complete each sentence. Write the word on the line.

| fork | horse | wore | adore | short |

11. Dad _____ a cap to the game.

12. Pack a _____ in the picnic basket.

13. It is just a _____ walk to the store.

14. We _____ our little kitten.

15. The _____ trotted into the barn.

Draw a line matching a word on the left to a rhyming word on the right.

16. cord   **a.** chore

17. form   **b.** storm

18. forecast   **c.** escort

19. support   **d.** bored

20. shore   **e.** contrast

Fluency Checklist

As you read the passage on the next page, be sure to keep the following things in mind to help you read with the appropriate rate, accuracy, and expression.

As you read, make sure you

☐ pause longer at a period or other ending punctuation.

☐ raise your voice at a question mark.

☐ use expression when you come to an exclamation point.

☐ pause at commas but not as long as you would at a period.

☐ think of the character and how he or she might say his or her words whenever you come to quotation marks.

☐ remember not to read so fast that someone listening cannot hear the individual words or make sense of what is being read.

☐ stop and reread something that does not make sense.

A Trip

Dad, Mom, and the kids went on a trip. They packed the van before they left. Dad grabbed bags until the van could fit no more.

Mom packed lunches, water, and snacks. She did not want to stop on the trip. The kids packed things to help them have fun for the long ride.

Traveling turned out to be fun! They went up and down hills. They went in and out of tunnels. Mom asked the kids if they wanted to sing. They said no thanks.

When the van stopped, the kids looked to see where they were. They saw a big forest. What would happen next? Dad jumped out of the van and started to unpack. The first things he grabbed were the tents. They would camp on this trip!

After the tents were finished, they set up their cots. The kids filled their packs. They wanted to explore the forest. Mom and Dad went with them.

They discovered lots of things in the forest. The best thing was seeing two elks by the water. It was a good first day of camping, and they had four more days to go.

Fluency • *Skills Practice*

/ā/ spelled *a* and *a_e*

FOCUS The /ā/ sound can be spelled with *a* and *a_e*.

PRACTICE Read the following words. Underline the *a* or *a_e* spelling pattern used in each word.

1. basic

2. rake

3. fade

4. staple

5. cane

6. favor

7. able

8. basis

Replace the underlined letters with the given letter or letters to create a rhyming word. The new word will have the same spelling for /ā/. Write the new word on the line.

9. f̲ able + t = _____

10. w̲ ave + g = _____

11. l̲ ake + f = _____

12. m̲ ade + f = _____

13. c̲ able + st = _____

14. v̲ ase + c = _____

APPLY Choose a word from the box below to complete each sentence. Write the word on the line.

bacon	taste	makes	trade	table	apron

15. My favorite breakfast is eggs and _____.

16. I will _____ you my apple for your banana.

17. Will you please set the _____ for dinner?

18. Aunt Kate _____ the best salads.

19. Dad wears an _____ when he is cooking.

20. Kathy can't wait to _____ the pasta.

Circle the correct spelling of each word.

21. baceon   bacon

22. fake   fak

23. date   daet

24. laybal   label

25. naem   name

26. rake   raek

/ī/ spelled *i* and *i_e*

FOCUS The /ī/ sound can be spelled with *i* and *i_e*.

PRACTICE Read the following words out loud.
Underline the *i* or *i_e* spelling pattern used in
each word.

1. idol   **5.** side

2. ride   **6.** pilot

3. item   **7.** hike

4. pipe   **8.** iris

**Write two sentences using any of the words spelled
with *i* and *i_e* from above.**

9. _____

_____

10. _____

_____

APPLY Choose a word from the box below to complete each sentence. Write the word on the line.

silent	time	dime	virus	kite	child

11. What _____ do you wake up?

12. A _____ is worth ten cents.

13. A _____ can make you feel sick.

14. Miles let his _____ rise in the wind.

15. The _____ sat on her mom's lap.

16. We must stay _____ when others are speaking.

Circle the correct spelling of each word.

17. blined   blind

18. fier   fire

19. wise   wis

20. ireon   iron

21. side   sid

22. rise   ries

/ō/ spelled o and o_e

> **FOCUS** The /ō/ sound can be spelled with o and o_e.

PRACTICE Replace the beginning letter of each word with one of the following letters to make a new rhyming word. Write the new word on the line. Use each letter one time.

j	d	r	w	m	s

1. no _____

2. nose _____

3. home _____

4. rove _____

5. host _____

6. poke _____

Use the pairs of words above to complete the following sentences. Write the words on the lines.

7. Use your _____ to smell the _____.

8. _____ parties will have a _____.

9. My mom said _____, _____ I cannot go to the park.

10. It's no _____ to get a _____ in the eye.

APPLY Read the word in the box. Then read the sentence. Change the word in the box to make a new rhyming word that will complete the sentence. Write the word on the line.

11. | cone | My dog loves to chew on his _____.

12. | toll | Mona put butter on the warm _____.

13. | fold | The man on the corner _____ hot dogs.

14. | roll | We dug a _____ in the backyard.

15. | bolt | Suddenly, the car stopped with a _____.

16. | nose | I watered the lawn with a _____.

Circle the correct spelling of each word.

17. sold   soled

18. oveal   oval

19. ohw   owe

20. pose   pos

21. toen   tone

22. old   oled

/ū/ spelled *u* and *u_e*

FOCUS The /ū/ sound can be spelled with *u* and *u_e*.

PRACTICE Read each sentence. Circle the word that correctly completes the sentence.

1. I don't like the _____ at the gas station.
fyumz   fumes

2. The _____ baby smiled at us.
cute   cut

3. Utah is one of the fifty _____ States of America.
Uneited   United

4. I _____ to give up.
refuse   refus

Circle the correct spelling of each word.

5. menu   menue

6. myusic   music

7. cueb   cube

8. fuse   fues

APPLY Use each word in the box in a sentence.
Write the sentence on the lines.

cute	humid	pupil	mule	mute	bugle

9. _____

_____

10. _____

_____

11. _____

_____

12. _____

_____

13. _____

_____

14. _____

_____

Long Vowels, Inflectional Endings
-er and -est

FOCUS
- The /ā/ sound can be spelled with *a* and *a_e*.
- The /ī/ sound can be spelled with *i* and *i_e*.
- The /ō/ sound can be spelled with *o* and *o_e*.
- The /ū/ sound can be spelled with *u* and *u_e*.
- The comparative ending *-er* compares two things.
- The superlative ending *-est* compares more than two things.

PRACTICE Underline the long-vowel spelling in each word.

1. blaze

2. music

3. robot

4. bite

5. pilot

6. fume

7. major

8. stroke

Circle the comparative or superlative adjective in each sentence.

9. Is it safer to walk or ride a bike?

10. This salsa is the mildest one we have made.

11. Lola has the whitest smile.

12. Jake's dog is older than mine.

APPLY Circle the correct spelling of each word.
Write the correct spelling on the line.

13. unit   uneit   _____

14. wild   wiled   _____

15. blaed   blade   _____

16. cuteer   cuter   _____

17. zon   zone   _____

18. post   poste   _____

19. cradel   cradle   _____

20. boldest   boledest   _____

21. hive   hiv   _____

22. confus   confuse   _____

Phonics • *Skills Practice*

/n/ spelled *kn_* and *gn;* /r/ spelled *wr_*

FOCUS
- The /n/ sound can be spelled with *kn_* and *gn.* When using the letters *kn* or *gn* together, you hear only the *n.*
- The /r/ sound can be spelled with *wr_.* When using the letters *wr* together, you hear only the *r.*

PRACTICE Add the letters as shown to form a word. Write the word on the line, and then read it aloud.

1. kn   +   ob   =   _____

2. gn   +   arl   =   _____

3. wr   +   inkle   =   _____

4. desi   +   gn   =   _____

5. kn   +   ife   =   _____

6. wr   +   ench   =   _____

APPLY Choose a word from the box to complete each sentence. Write the word on the line.

knelt	knack	wrap	gnat	wreck	knot	align	wrong

7. The string is tangled in a _____.

8. Braces help teeth _____ properly.

9. The catcher _____ in the dirt and waited for a pitch.

10. Mr. Miller lets us correct an answer if it is _____.

11. A _____ buzzed around the picnic table.

12. Thick fog caused the cars to _____.

13. I can help _____ the presents.

14. Amy is a singer with a _____ for high notes.

Phonics • *Skills Practice*

/ē/ spelled e and e_e

FOCUS The /ē/ sound can be spelled with e and e_e.

PRACTICE Read each sentence. Circle the word with /ē/. Write e or e_e on the line for the /ē/ spelling pattern of each word you circle.

1. Did you complete the chores? _____

2. Mom's present is a secret. _____

Choose a word from the box that makes sense in the sentence. Write the word on the line.

3. We _____ math class after lunch.

Mr. Jones showed us a problem.

_____ helped us find the answer.

before
He
began

4. Jessica is a runner.

_____ wins a lot of races.

Jessica likes to _____.

compete
rewind
She

APPLY Look at the pairs of words below. Choose the correctly spelled word that will complete the sentence. Write the word on the line.

5. Gene is sick and has a _fever_.
(fever, fevr)

6. An _athlete_ is a person who plays sports.
(athlet, athlete)

7. We will take a _pretest_ before the lesson.
(preetest, pretest)

8. _these_ books belong to Lena.
(These, Thes)

9. The sidewalk is made of _concrete_.
(concret, concrete)

10. Steve wants to _Be_ a doctor.
(bee, be)

11. Two girls will _compete_ in the tennis match.
(compete, compet)

12. The sign says "_Beware_ of Dog!"
(Bewear, Beware)

13. The Clarks will _Remodel_ their kitchen next spring.
(reemodel, remodel)

14. Victor likes the school's new _theme_ song.
(theme, them)

/ē/ spelled *ee* and *ea*
Homographs and Homophones

FOCUS The /ē/ sound can be spelled with ee and *ea*.

PRACTICE Read the words in the box aloud. Then follow the directions below.

dream	week	feet	cheat

Write the words with /ē/ spelled like *leaf*.

1. _____   2. _____

Write the words with /ē/ spelled like *need*.

3. _____   4. _____

APPLY Write a word from the box to complete each sentence.

5. Friday is the best day of the _____.

6. Reed's _____ is to become a pilot.

7. It is not fair to _____ on a test.

8. These socks keep Dena's _____ warm.

/ē/ spelled ee, e_e, ea, and e

FOCUS The /ē/ sound can be spelled with e, e_e, ee, and ea.

PRACTICE Underline the /ē/ spellings in the words below. Some words have two spellings for /ē/.

1. beagle

2. between

3. legal

4. seaweed

5. delete

6. complete

7. resubmit

8. extreme

9. reheat

10. depend

APPLY Choose the word that completes each sentence. Write the word on the line.

11. Eve wants a _____. But what does _____
(tree, treat)   (she, me)

_____ to eat? Will she have _____?
(perfect, prefer)   (pants, peanuts)

Or will she have something _____?
(sweet, sweat)

12. The talent show is only two _____ away.
(weaks, weeks)

Zeke can juggle _____ bags.
(been, bean)

He also has a _____ puppet.
(zebra, zero)

Zeke can _____ without moving his lips.
(speck, speak)

It _____ like the puppet talks!
(seems, seams)

Fluency Checklist

As you read the passage on the next page, be sure to keep the following things in mind to help you read with the appropriate rate, accuracy, and expression.

As you read, make sure you

- [ ] pause longer at a period or other ending punctuation.

- [ ] raise your voice at a question mark.

- [ ] use expression when you come to an exclamation point.

- [ ] pause at commas but not as long as you would at a period.

- [ ] think of the character and how he or she might say his or her words whenever you come to quotation marks.

- [ ] remember not to read so fast that someone listening cannot hear the individual words or make sense of what is being read.

- [ ] stop and reread something that does not make sense.

A Wreck

Jean Smith just turned seven years old. A sign in her yard read, "Jean is seven!"

Jean's gift was a bike! It came in a huge box wrapped in white and green paper. Mom and Dad set the box in the yard. Jean knelt next to it and began to open it.

Jean was shocked! Jean did not see a bike. She just saw parts of a bike. She saw wheels and tires, green fenders, steel bars and pipes, knobs, pedals, and a seat. But she did not see a bike!

"That is not a bike!" Jean said. "It is a bike wreck!"

Both Mom and Dad chuckled. "No, it is not a wreck," said Mom.

"We just need to put these parts together." Dad added.

Mom held a paper that had been in the box. "We will read this. It will tell us how to do it," she told Jean.

After Mom read the paper, Mom and Dad got a wrench, a hammer, and other things. Jean helped Mom and Dad put the bike together. It did not take much time to finish.

The three Smiths looked at the green bike shining in the sun. "It looks pretty good for a wreck!" Dad said.

"I was wrong! It is not a wreck! It is my bike! I bet it is faster than most bikes!" Jean said.

Jean gave Mom and Dad a huge hug and said, "Thanks, Mom and Dad!"

/ā/ spelled *ai_* and *_ay*

FOCUS • The /ā/ sound can be spelled with *ai_* and *_ay*.
• Another letter follows the *ai* spelling.
• Another letter comes before the *ay* spelling.

PRACTICE Read the words in the box aloud.

aim	paint	okay	display
rain	away	waist	maybe

Write the words with /ā/ spelled like *aid*.

1. _____   3. _____

2. _____   4. _____

Write the words with /ā/ spelled like *way*.

5. _____   7. _____

6. _____   8. _____

APPLY Choose a word from the box to complete each sentence. Write the word on the line.

bait	braid	holiday	sway	explain
away	wait	spray	drain	maybe

9. Thanksgiving is my favorite _____.

10. Dana wears her hair in a _____.

11. The teacher will _____ our homework.

12. Nicole put _____ on her fishing hook.

13. Pull the plug to let the water _____ out of the sink.

14. Hank has to _____ for his turn on the swingset.

15. Keep the cat and dog _____ from each other.

16. _____ I will see you at the parade.

17. The tall trees _____ in the wind.

18. _____ the car with water to wash off all of the suds.

Phonics • *Skills Practice*

/ā/ spelled *a*, *a_e*, *ai_*, and *_ay*

FOCUS The /ā/ sound can be spelled with *a*, *a_e*, *ai_*, and *_ay*.

PRACTICE Read the word in the box. Then read the sentence. Change the beginning of the word in the box to make a new rhyming word that completes the sentence.

1. | same | A wild animal is not _tamed_.

2. | pay | Mixing black and white makes _grey_.

3. | fair | Shoes come as a _Lair_.

4. | tray | The barn is filled with bales of _hay_.

5. | whale | The store is having a big _sale_.

6. | came | Write your _name_ at the top of your paper.

7. | gain | Let's ride the _thain_ into the city.

8. | sway | We like to _way_ kickball at the park.

9. | save | A big _____ crashed on the beach.

10. | stair | Pam likes to sit in the rocking _chair_.

APPLY Read each sentence. Circle the word that correctly completes the sentence.

11. James wants to _____ the leaves into a big pile.
   a. rake   **b.** rayke   **c.** rak   **d.** raik

12. If the _____ does not stop, we can play inside.
   a. raine   **b.** rane   **c.** rain   **d.** rayn

13. We made _____ pots in art class.
   a. claiy   **b.** clay   **c.** claye   **d.** clae

14. The _____ is locked each night at 9:00.
   a. gayt   **b.** gait   **c.** geyt   **d.** gate

15. Do you like red or green _____?
   a. grapes   **b.** graips   **c.** graypes   **d.** greyps

16. A monkey has a _____, but an ape does not.
   a. tayl   **b.** tael   **c.** taile   **d.** tail

17. Mother's Day is in the month of _____.
   a. Mai   **b.** Mae   **c.** May   **d.** Mey

18. A _____ of black horses pulled the wagon.
   a. payr   **b.** pair   **c.** pare   **d.** pear

19. We cannot _____ on the sidewalk.
   a. skat   **b.** skait   **c.** skate   **d.** skayt

20. Get a pump to _____ the flat tire.
   a. inflate   **b.** inflait   **c.** inflat   **d.** inflayt

Phonics • *Skills Practice*

/ē/ spelled _ie_, _y, and _ey

FOCUS
- The /ē/ sound can be spelled with _ie_, _y, and _ey.
- The _ie_ spelling pattern is usually found in the middle of a word.
- The _y and _ey spelling patterns are usually found at the end of a word.

PRACTICE Read each word and underline the /ē/ spelling pattern.

1. shield

2. alley

3. pretty

4. many

5. valley

6. grief

Choose one of the /ē/ spelling patterns listed above to complete each word. Write the letter or letters to complete each word.

7. lad_____

8. ch_____f

9. donk_____

10. y_____ld

11. cit_____

12. barl_____

APPLY Read the sentence. Choose the word that completes the sentence. Write the word on the line.

13. A _____ stole the gold ring.
(thief, thefe, theyfe)

14. My glass of milk is now _____.
(emptie, empty, emptee)

15. We watched the _____ swing on a rope.
(monkie, monkee, monkey)

16. Henry planted corn in the _____.
(feeld, field, feyld)

17. How much _____ is in the piggy bank?
(money, monie, mony)

18. Kathy felt _____ to win the raffle.
(lucky, luckie, luckey)

19. The _____ slept in her crib.
(babey, baby, babie)

20. Jerry likes _____ in his tea.
(honie, hony, honey)

21. Can you help me pick some _____ today?
(berrys, berries, bareys)

22. Will you read this _____ with me?
(storie, storey, story)

Phonics • *Skills Practice*

/ē/ spelled e, e_e, ee, ea, _ie_, _y, and _ey

> **FOCUS**
> - Long vowels sound like their names.
> - The /ē/ sound can be spelled with e, e_e, ee, ea, _ie_, _y, and _ey.

PRACTICE Unscramble the words below. Write the word on the first line and the /ē/ spelling pattern on the second line.

1. i d l f e _____ _____

2. e e n v _____ _____

3. z e e r e b _____ _____

4. y c z a r _____ _____

5. e r a h c _____ _____

6. y r l o l t e _____ _____

7. l d t e e e _____ _____

8. e e r f _____ _____

9. i o p s n e _____ _____

10. s y a e _____ _____

APPLY Circle the correct spelling for each word.

11. refund   reefund

12. finalley   finally

13. reason   reeson

14. cheif   chief

15. screan   screen

Choose a word from above to complete each sentence. Write the word on the line.

16. We looked for days and _____ found the lost ring.

17. The fire department promoted a new _____.

18. Did Julie give a _____ for being absent?

19. Please wipe the _____ with a soft cloth to keep it clean.

20. The store will _____ your money or let you make an exchange.

/ā/ and /ē/ spellings

FOCUS
- The /ā/ sound can be spelled with *a*, *a_e*, *ai_*, and *_ay*.
- The /ē/ sound can be spelled with *e*, *e_e*, *ee*, *ea*, *_ie_*, *_y*, and *_ey*.

PRACTICE Underline the /ā/ or /ē/ spelling pattern in each word. Write the pattern, and then write a new word that has the same spelling pattern. The words do not have to rhyme.

1. leap _____ _____

2. respond _____ _____

3. raise _____ _____

4. play _____ _____

5. athlete _____ _____

6. major _____ _____

7. flake _____ _____

8. bunnies _____ _____

9. jersey _____ _____

10. sweet _____ _____

APPLY Choose a word from the box to complete each sentence. Write the word on the line.

| detail | squeaky | prepare | referee | daydream | shield |

11. The shopping cart has a _____ wheel.

12. The _____ stopped the game due to rain.

13. A hat and glasses will _____ your face from the sun.

14. A story is more interesting with lots of _____.

15. When my mind wanders I _____ about the beach.

16. We begin to _____ dinner at 5:00.

Draw a line to connect the rhyming words.

17. played   delete

18. repeat   cheater

19. lazy   quirky

20. peeled   made

21. turkey   daisy

22. meter   yield

/f/ spelled *ph*, /m/ spelled _*mb*, and silent letters

FOCUS
- /f/ can be spelled with *ph*.
- /m/ can be spelled with _*mb*. When using the letters *mb* together, the *b* is silent and you hear only the /m/ sound.
- Silent letters in a word are not heard when the word is pronounced.

PRACTICE Add the letters shown to form a word. Write the word on the line, then read it aloud.

1. ph + oto = _Photo_

2. li + mb = _Limb_

3. co + mb = _comb_

4. gra + ph = _graph_

5. nu + mb = _numb_

6. ph + ase = _Phase_

Read each word. Circle the letter or letters that are silent.

7. debt

8. hour

9. science

10. character

11. wrestle

12. adjust

APPLY Read the sentence. Choose the word that
completes the sentence. Write the word on the line.

13. My _____ was ringing all day.
(fone, phone,)

14. Maddie loves the _____ of this perfume.
(sent, scent)

15. Dad told us to _____ for the timer to beep.
(listen, lissen)

16. Mr. White called a _____ to fix the clogged drain.
(plumer, plumber)

17. A chart is made of rows and _____.
(columns, columbs)

18. Holly helped her little sister learn the _____.
(alphabet, alfabet)

19. A bridge connects the _____ to the mainland.
(iland, island)

20. Jonah pressed the button with his _____.
(thumb, thum)

21. A _____ makes a comparison between two things.
(metafor, metaphor)

22. Stephanie _____ up the ladder to the slide.
(climes, climbs)

/s/ spelled *ce*, *ci_*, and *cy*

FOCUS The /s/ sound can be spelled *ce*, *ci_*, and *cy*.

PRACTICE Read each word aloud. Underline the spelling pattern that makes /s/.

1. ice

2. policy

3. pencil

4. center

5. lacy

6. city

7. trace

8. civil

Use a word from the box to complete each sentence. Write the word on the line.

rice	circus	fancy	fleece

9. Clowns make people happy at the _circus_.

10. Let's eat at a _fancy_ restaurant on your birthday.

11. Grace wore her _fleece_ coat to practice.

12. The beans and _rice_ taste good!

APPLY Choose a word from the box that makes sense in the sentence. Write the word on the line.

13. We went out to eat dinner.

The pizza was in the shape

of a _____.

I ate three _____.

> circle
> fancy
> slices

14. Jack's _____ loves

to read. Her favorite subject

is _____.

> percent
> science
> niece

15. Rebecca's family lives in

the _____. When they need

_____ to run, they go

to the park.

> city
> race
> space

16. Cole cannot _____

on his work. He is _____

about going to Ellen's party.

> concern
> concentrate
> excited

Phonics • *Skills Practice*

/j/ spelled *ge* and *gi_*

FOCUS The /j/ sound can be spelled *ge* and *gi_*.

PRACTICE Read each word aloud. Underline the spelling pattern that makes /j/.

1. rage
2. logic
3. giant
4. gentle

5. cringe
6. giraffe
7. orange
8. general

Read the words in the box. Write each word under the correct heading.

digest	frigid	tragic	twinge	general	ginger

ge	*gi_*
9. _____	12. _____
10. _____	13. _____
11. _____	14. _____

APPLY Read the sentence. Choose the word that correctly completes the sentence. Write the word on the line.

15. Angela left a _____ for you.
(message, messig)

16. The car's _____ needs a tune-up.
(enjine, engine)

17. The number 153 has three _____.
(digits, digets)

18. Can you _____ what it's like to be a bird?
(imagen, imagine)

19. We stayed in a _____ by the lake.
(cottage, cottij)

20. Be very _____ with the bunnies.
(gintle, gentle)

21. The glass vase is quite _____.
(fragel, fragile)

22. Let's plant a _____ garden.
(vegetable, vegitable)

23. Marge ordered a _____ beverage.
(larj, large)

24. The cash _____ prints our receipt.
(register, regester)

Phonics • *Skills Practice*

/ī/ spelled _igh, _ie, and _y

> **FOCUS** The /ī/ sound can be spelled _igh, _ie, and _y.

PRACTICE Unscramble the following words. Write the word on the first line and the /ī/ spelling on the second line.

1. k y s _____   _____

2. r i f e d _____   _____

3. g t h i t _____   _____

4. s i s p e _____   _____

5. l e t s y _____   _____

Write three sentences using words from above.

6. _____

_____

7. _____

_____

8. _____

_____

APPLY Choose a word from the box to complete
each sentence. Write the word on the line.

bright	lie	why	type	might	applied

9. If you sleep in, you _____ miss the bus.

10. _____ is the alarm ringing?

11. Lilah wore a _____ yellow rain jacket.

12. Brian _____ for a job at the market.

13. Telling a _____ is not a way to solve problems.

14. What _____ of pet is your favorite?

**Draw a line matching a word on the left to a rhyming
word on the right.**

15. try   **a.** high

16. night   **b.** fight

17. sighs   **c.** dry

18. pie   **d.** dries

/ī/ spelled *i, i_e, _igh, _ie,* and *_y*

> **FOCUS** The /ī/ sound can be spelled *i, i_e, _igh, _ie,* and *_y.*

PRACTICE Underline the /ī/ spelling pattern in each of the following words.

1. idea
2. criticize
3. flies
4. title

5. light
6. incline
7. China
8. shy

Change the first letter or letters of each word to make a new rhyming word. Write the word on the line.

9. bride _____

10. kind _____

11. child _____

12. flight _____

13. tie _____

14. by _____

APPLY Choose a word from the box to complete each sentence. Write the word on the line.

high	beside	diet	quiet	prize
unties	shiny	why	trial	advice

15. We must be _____ in the library.

16. Bo won the _____ for best costume.

17. Is the top shelf too _____ for you to reach?

18. Jess is on a dairy-free _____ .

19. _____ do you like pizza so much?

20. Whenever I need help, Uncle Hal always gives me really good _____ .

21. Mark always _____ his shoes before he takes them off.

22. The twins like to sit _____ each other.

23. The judge wore a black robe during the _____ .

24. Sally polished the car until it was _____ .

Phonics • *Skills Practice*

A Rainy Day

Rain fell again. Mike told Mom, "This is so much rain! It has been raining day and night."

"Well, farm fields need rain. Rain will help my garden," said Mom.

"But, Mom, this much rain is boring!" said Mike.

For a while, Mike played different kinds of games on Mom's laptop in the den. But that quickly felt boring, as well. Then Mike just looked out at the yard. He gazed at the gray sky. The rain had stopped a bit. Now there was even a gopher on top of the fence. How did it climb up there?

Then Mike gazed at the street. Thanks to the rain, there was a tiny stream of water running down the side of the cement curb. The water rushed to a rusty drain. Mike saw the stream carry leaves down the street. Most leaves fell in the drain. Only some leaves did not. Why did those leaves escape the drain?

Before he realized it, Mike was thinking about what it might be like to ride a leaf on the current. If he were tiny like a leaf, could he slide over that drain and not drop in?

Mike pretended he sat on the center of a leaf. He tightly held its edges while it spun around in the rushing stream. Mike twisted his body left and right. He tried to control the leaf! He had to lead it around wide gaps in the drain! He was not afraid. "I believe I can do it," Mike said to himself.

Soon Mike felt wet and cold! Fresh rain hit his face. He felt water rush over his leaf's edges!

Suddenly, the giant drain was right there! With great skill, Mike turned his leaf this way and that. Would the leaf fall into the drain's gaps? Or would Mike safely lead his leaf past those gaps?

Look out! Mike came close to slipping off his leaf! As he hung on, it spun and spun. Oh no! But Mike's leaf spun past the drain's gaps! It was not easy, but Mike made it! He was safe! As his leaf glided gently down the street, Mike yelled, "Yes!"

Mom came into the den. "Mike, did that yell mean rain is not boring?" she asked.

Mike grinned and said, "No, Mom. It means my daydreams are not boring!"

Fluency • *Skills Practice*

/ō/ spelled _ow, oa_, o, and o_e

> **FOCUS** The /ō/ sound can be spelled _ow, oa_, o, and o_e.

PRACTICE Use the equations to add (+) and remove (−) letters to create different /ō/ words.

1. glow   − g + f   = _____   − f + b   = _____

2. poke   − p + j   = _____   − j + sp   = _____

3. grow   − g + c   = _____   − c + th   = _____

4. road   − r + t   = _____   − t + l   = _____

5. host   − h + p   = _____   − p + m   = _____

6. coat   − c + b   = _____   − b + m   = _____

Write two sentences using words from the equations above. Underline the /ō/ spelling pattern in each word you choose.

7. _____

_____

8. _____

_____

APPLY Choose a word from the box to complete each sentence.

hollow	oak	bone	throat	mow
oval	vote	frozen	yellow	loaf

9. We can ice-skate on the _____ pond.

10. Rabbits made a nest in the _____ log.

11. Anna gets paid to _____ the grass.

12. Luke has a fever and a sore _____.

13. We _____ for class president next week.

14. The warm _____ of bread smells wonderful.

15. Let's rest under the giant _____ tree.

16. Barkley hid his _____ in the backyard.

17. The racetrack has an _____ shape.

18. The large, _____ bus stopped to pick us up.

Phonics • *Skills Practice*

Compound Words, Synonyms, and Antonyms

FOCUS
- A **compound word** is made when two words are put together to make a new word. For example: gold + fish = goldfish
- **Synonyms** are words that are similar in meaning. *Tired* and *sleepy* are synonyms.
- **Antonyms** are words that are opposite in meaning. *Bad* and *good* are antonyms.

PRACTICE **Combine the words below to make a compound word. Write the new word on the line.**

1. table + cloth = _Table cloth_

2. home + work = _home work_

3. lady + bug = _ladybug_

Draw a line to match each word to its *synonym.*

4. choose   **a.** giggle

5. ill   **b.** select

6. laugh   **c.** sick

Draw a line to match each word to its *antonym.*

7. before   **a.** work

8. over   **b.** after

9. play   **c.** under

APPLY Fill in each blank with a compound word.

10. A bath for a bird is a _____.

11. A pot to put tea in is a _____.

12. Light that comes from the sun is _____.

13. A cone that comes from a pine tree is a _____.

14. A cake that is made in a cup is a _____.

Write a synonym for the word in parentheses ( ) to complete the sentence.

15. (angry) Mr. Banks was _____ that we broke the window.

16. (seat) Sit on the _____ next to Tori.

17. (shout) I had to _____ so Dad could hear me over the lawnmower.

Write an antonym for the word in parentheses ( ) to complete the sentence.

18. (gloomy) Lots of people go to the park on a

_____ day.

19. (last) We were _____ in line to get tickets for the show.

20. (close) The weather is warm enough for me to

_____ my window.

/ū/ spelled _ew, _ue, u, and u_e

> **FOCUS** The /ū/ sound can be spelled _ew, _ue, u, and u_e.

PRACTICE Read the following words aloud.

cue	pew	humor	compute
unit	amuse	value	curfew

Write the words with /ū/ spelled like *hue*.

1. _____   2. _____

Write the words with /ū/ spelled like *few*.

3. _____   4. _____

Write the words with /ū/ spelled like *music*.

5. _____   6. _____

Write the words with /ū/ spelled like *cute*.

7. _____   8. _____

APPLY Circle the word with /ū/ in each sentence. Write the word and its /ū/ spelling pattern on the lines.

9. Lexi is always home before her curfew.

   _____   _____

10. Did Max use all of the cups?

   _____   _____

11. A police officer came to the rescue!

   _____   _____

12. Was the stolen art returned to the museum?

   _____   _____

13. A sunny day is good for a barbecue.

   _____   _____

14. Water spewed from the broken hose.

   _____   _____

15. Gus gave his chums a huge hug.

   _____   _____

16. Angela refuses to give up.

   _____   _____

Multiple-Meaning Words

> ***FOCUS*** **Multiple-meaning words** are spelled and pronounced the same but have different meanings. **Example:**
> **bark** Meaning 1: the sound a dog makes
> Meaning 2: the outer coating on a tree

PRACTICE **Use the multiple-meaning words below to complete the sentences. Use each word twice.**

kind	last	sink

1. Hugo is always _____. What _____ of pizza do you like?

2. A hole in the boat will cause it to _____. The dishes in the _____ still need to be washed.

3. December is the _____ month of the year. These sneakers will not _____ another year.

APPLY **Read the two meanings for a multiple-meaning word. Write the word on the line.**

4. a deep, round dish for holding liquids **or** to play a game by knocking down pins with a ball _____

5. to cram or wedge into something **or** a type of jelly _____

6. a water bird with a bill and webbed feet that quacks **or** to lower or bend down quickly _____

Homophones

FOCUS Homophones are words that are pronounced the same but have different spellings and meanings. **Example:** I <u>see</u> a dolphin swimming in the <u>sea</u>.

PRACTICE Use these homophones to complete the sentences.

we'll	rowed	cents
wheel	road	sense

7. A gumball costs 50 _____. Use your _____ of smell to sniff the perfume.

8. The wagon won't roll if it's missing a _____. If we study tonight, _____ be ready for the test tomorrow.

9. A car stopped at the side of the _____. Henry and Rachel _____ their boat to shore.

APPLY Read the two meanings for a pair of homophones. Write the homophones on the lines.

10. the number after seven _____

   past tense of *eat* _____

11. the opposite of *yes* _____

   to understand _____

12. using the voice to be heard _____

   to be permitted _____

/ō/ spelled _ow, oa_, o and o_e

> **FOCUS** The /ō/ sound can be spelled _ow, oa_, o, and o_e.

PRACTICE Read the following words aloud.
Underline the /ō/ spelling or spellings in each word.

1. rodeo
2. overflow
3. ozone

4. explode
5. roadblock
6. boatload

APPLY Write one of the words from above to complete
each sentence.

7. Don't let the bath water _____ from the tub!

8. Cars were forced to turn around at the _____.

9. Barrel racing is an event at the _____.

10. The _____ layer helps protect life on Earth.

11. That volcano will _____ soon.

12. We bought a _____ of clothes during the sale.

/ū/ spelled _ew, _ue, u, and u_e

> **FOCUS** The /ū/ sound can be spelled _ew, _ue, u,
> and u_e.

PRACTICE Read the following word pairs.
Circle the word with /ū/.

13. full   fuel

14. abuse   abrupt

15. continent   continue

16. humid   hummed

17. volume   volunteer

18. cupped   cupid

APPLY Draw a line to connect the rhyming words.

19. skews   **a.** venue

20. few   **b.** contribute

21. menu   **c.** pew

22. distribute   **d.** fuse

Phonics • *Skills Practice*

Prefix *dis-*

> **FOCUS**
> - A **prefix** is added to the beginning of a word and changes the meaning of that word.
> - The prefix *dis-* means "the opposite of" or "not."
>   **Example:** dis + comfort = discomfort (the lack or opposite of comfort)

PRACTICE Add the prefix *dis-* to the base words below. Write the new word on the first line. Then write the meaning of the new word.

Base Word	New Word	New Meaning
1. advantage	_____	_____
2. appear	_____	_____
3. order	_____	_____
4. respect	_____	_____

APPLY Write two sentences using the new words from above.

5. _____

_____

6. _____

_____

Prefix *un-*

FOCUS
- A **prefix** is added to the beginning of a word and changes the meaning of that word.
- The prefix *un-* means "the opposite of" or "not."
  Example: un + happy = unhappy (not happy)

PRACTICE Add the prefix *un-* to the base words below. Write the new word on the first line. Then write the meaning of the new word.

Base Word	New Word	New Meaning
7. buckle	_____	_____
8. ripe	_____	_____
9. common	_____	_____
10. stuck	_____	_____
11. real	_____	_____

APPLY Fill in the blank with the prefix *dis-* or *un-* to create a new word that makes sense in the sentence.

12. Joe used a key to _____lock the safe.

13. We were _____interested in the boring speech.

14. It is _____safe for the wires to be

_____connected.

/o͞o/ spelled oo

FOCUS The /o͞o/ sound can be spelled oo.

PRACTICE Read the sentence. Change the word in the box to make a new rhyming word. Write the new word on the line.

1. | broom | The bride and _____ had a fancy wedding.

2. | moon | We usually eat lunch at _____.

3. | noodle | The little _____ is chasing its tail.

4. | pool | Put on a jacket if the air is too _____.

5. | mood | How much _____ did you pack for the picnic?

6. | boots | A plant's _____ hold it in the dirt.

7. | gloom | Hal's roses _____ in the summer.

8. | goof | Rain leaked in from a hole in the _____.

APPLY Choose a word from the box to complete each sentence. Write the word on the line.

moon	scoop	bedroom	loose	boots
cartoon	zoomed	tools	pool	too

9. Matt prefers to study in his _____.

10. A dentist uses _____ to clean and fix teeth.

11. Let's watch the _____ with a dog named Scooby Doo.

12. The rocket _____ into the air.

13. A _____ ring might slip off your finger.

14. _____ some food into the cat's dish.

15. Sally needs a warm pair of _____ for the winter.

16. Does Nick's swimming _____ have a diving board?

17. I will go to the party, and Tess will come _____.

18. A full _____ can light up the night.

Prefix *non-*

FOCUS
- A **prefix** is added to the beginning of a word and changes the meaning of that word.
- The prefix *non-* means "the opposite of" or "not."
  Example: non + human = nonhuman (not human)

PRACTICE Add the prefix *non-* to the base words below. Write the new word on the first line. Then write the meaning of the new word.

Base Word	New Word	New Meaning
1. living	_____	_____
2. fat	_____	_____
3. fiction	_____	_____
4. sense	_____	_____

APPLY Write two sentences using the new words from above.

5. _____

_____

6. _____

_____

Prefix *re-*

FOCUS
- A **prefix** is added to the beginning of a word and changes the meaning of that word.
- The prefix *re-* means "again" or "back."
  Example: re + play = replay (play again or play back)

PRACTICE Add the prefix *re-* to the base words below. Write the new word on the first line. Then write the meaning of the new word.

Base Word	New Word	New Meaning
7. call	_____	_____
8. trace	_____	_____
9. turn	_____	_____
10. do	_____	_____
11. write	_____	_____

APPLY Fill in the blank with the prefix *non-* or *re-* to create a new word that makes sense in the sentence.

12. Bree wants to _____ join the swim team next summer.

13. Josh uses _____ toxic cleaners that do not harm his skin.

14. We will _____ decorate the room after we _____ paint the walls.

Word Analysis • *Skills Practice*

/o͞o/ spelled *u, u_e, _ew,* and *_ue*

> **FOCUS** The /o͞o/ sound can be spelled with *u, u_e, _ew,* and *_ue.*

PRACTICE Use the words in the box to fill in the blanks.

rumor	stew	utility	cashew	tune
drew	ruin	clue	flute	pursue

Write the words with /o͞o/ spelled like *grew.*

1. _____   3. _____

2. _____

Write the words with /o͞o/ spelled like *rude.*

4. _____   5. _____

Write the words with /o͞o/ spelled like *due.*

6. _____   7. _____

Write the words with /o͞o/ spelled like *truth.*

8. _____   10. _____

9. _____

APPLY Replace the underlined letter or letters to create a rhyming word. The new word will have the same spelling pattern for $/\overline{oo}/$.

11. <u>cl</u>ue + tr = _____

12. <u>n</u>ew + ch = _____

13. <u>b</u>lue + g = _____

14. <u>co</u>nclude + i = _____

Read the paragraph. Circle the misspelled words. Write the words correctly on the blanks below.

Summer begins in the month of Jewn. Lots of nue blossoms appear on trees and plants. People swim in cool, bloo pools. They listen to tewns as they cut the grass. Other summer activities inclood hiking and camping. Some like to brue iced tea and then sip it on the porch.

15. _____

16. _____

17. _____

18. _____

19. _____

20. _____

Prefix *pre-*

FOCUS
- A **prefix** is added to the beginning of a word and changes the meaning of that word.
- The prefix *pre-* means "before in place, time, or order." **Example:** pre + made = premade (made ahead of time)

PRACTICE Add the prefix *pre-* to the base words below. Write the new word on the first line. Then write the meaning of the new word.

Base Word	New Word	New Meaning
1. cooked	_____	_____
2. pay	_____	_____
3. pack	_____	_____
4. game	_____	_____

APPLY Write two sentences using the new words from above.

5. _____

_____

6. _____

_____

Prefix *mis-*

FOCUS
- A **prefix** is added to the beginning of a word and changes the meaning of that word.
- The prefix *mis-* means "bad," "wrong," or "incorrectly." **Example:** mis + judge = misjudge (to judge incorrectly)

PRACTICE Add the prefix *re-* to the base words below. Write the new word on the first line. Then write the meaning of the new word.

Base Word	New Word	New Meaning
7. count	_____	_____
8. behave	_____	_____
9. match	_____	_____
10. place	_____	_____

APPLY Fill in the blank with the prefix *pre-* or *mis-* to create a new word that makes sense in the sentence.

11. Kaylee felt like a _____ fit and didn't have fun at camp.

12. Dad _____ arranged for a cab to pick us up at the airport.

13. If you _____ soak the shirt before washing, the stain might come out.

14. Toby would never _____ treat his pets.

Word Analysis • *Skills Practice*

Ocean Life

Did you know that ocean water has salt in it? Thousands of living things make the ocean their home. Plants and animals have parts that help them live in the saltwater. Some creatures are tiny, but the largest animal on Earth lives in the ocean too!

Kelp is a kind of plant that lives in the ocean. It can grow very tall underwater. It is very different from land plants. It does not have a trunk like trees. Kelp is not delicate though. It has strong stems that can move in the water. Parts that trap air bubbles help this plant float. Then it can get closer to the sunlight above the water.

Many kinds of plants live in the ocean. Some plants are large like kelp. Other plants are so tiny that you need a microscope to see them! These tiny plants float in the water. They like to live in cool water. They need a lot of sunlight to live.

The bottom of the ocean does not get much sunlight. It is very dark and cold. One kind of fish that lives there glows like a flashlight! The glowing part helps the fish find food. This part can be bad though. Sometimes it is hard for this fish to hide from other animals.

Living things in Earth's oceans help each other. A sea anemone is an animal that lives in the ocean. It can sting other animals. It does not harm one kind of fish though. The clownfish shares its food with the anemone. A sea anemone is a protective home for the clownfish.

Another ocean animal is a giant octopus. It is big and has eight arms! It is a shy, but very smart animal. An octopus can change the coloration of its body. Then it can blend in with parts of the ocean. The camouflage helps the octopus get food and hide from other animals.

The largest animal on Earth is the blue whale. It eats tiny animals. During the summer, blue whales like to live in cool ocean water. A lot of food can be found there. During the winter, blue whales live in warm ocean water. Baby blue whales are born there.

The ocean is home to many plants and animals. Scientists continue to learn more and more about the ocean every year. You should too!

/oo/ spelled oo

FOCUS The /oo/ sound is spelled with *oo*. The *oo* spelling pattern is usually found in the middle of a word.

PRACTICE Use the letters in parentheses ( ) to write a word on the line with the *oo* spelling pattern.

1. (b, k) _____

2. (f, t) _____

3. (w, d) _____

4. (h, k) _____

5. (h, d) _____

6. (c, k) _____

7. (s, t, d) _____

8. (s, h, k) _____

9. (l, k) _____

10. (w, l) _____

APPLY Read each word, and then write a new rhyming word on the line.

11. book _____

12. hood _____

13. shook _____

14. look _____

15. stood _____

Complete each sentence by writing one of the above words on the blank line.

16. I like to read a _____ before I go to sleep.

17. My jacket has a _____ for cold or rainy weather.

18. Charlie _____ at the bus stop with his friends.

19. The doctor is taking a _____ at Anna's sore throat.

20. The mayor _____ hands with all of her supporters.

Comparative Ending -er, Superlative Ending -est, and Irregular Comparatives

> **FOCUS**
> - The **comparative ending** -er shows a comparison between two things.
> - The **superlative ending** -est shows a comparison among three or more things.
> - Some words that show comparison do not follow the usual patterns of adding -er or -est. These words are **irregular comparatives**.

PRACTICE Add -er to the following words. Write each new word on the line.

1. clean _____

2. mad _____

3. easy _____

4. dark _____

Add -est to the following words. Write each new word on the line.

5. bright _____

6. funny _____

7. smooth _____

8. wise _____

Draw a line to match the comparative form to its superlative form.

9. worse   **a.** best

10. more   **b.** most

11. less   **c.** worst

12. better   **d.** least

APPLY Circle the correct word to complete each sentence.

13. Lance's bike is (newer   newest) than Henry's.

14. Mr. Jones raked the (biggest   bigger) pile of leaves on our street.

15. The lunchroom is (noisyest   noisiest) on Fridays.

16. Which of these two books costs (less   least)?

17. This feels like the (hottest   hotest) day of the year!

18. Nate's hair is (curlier   curlyer) on rainy days.

19. Kate said that was the (worse   worst) movie she'd ever seen!

20. The public pool is (deepest   deeper) than our swimming pool.

21. The new washer works much (best   better) than the old one did.

22. Zack has the (least   less) amount of absences this year.

23. I thought the sequel was (least   less) exciting than the first movie.

24. The car looked a lot (shiniest   shinier) after we waxed it.

Word Analysis • *Skills Practice*

/ow/ spelled ow and ou_

> **FOCUS** The /ow/ sound can be spelled ow and ou_.

PRACTICE Read the sentence. Change the word in the box to make a new rhyming word that completes the sentence. Write the new word on the line.

1. | brown | The queen's _____ is made of solid gold and real jewels.

2. | found | Worms and other animals live beneath the _____.

3. | couch | A baby kangaroo travels in its mother's _____.

4. | town | The _____ on Eric's face told us he was quite unhappy.

5. | chowder | Suki sprinkles _____ in her boots to keep her feet dry.

6. | sound | We bake pies in a _____ pan and cakes rectangular pan.

APPLY Read the sentence. Circle the word that
completes each sentence. Write the word on the line.

7. Use a hammer to _____ the nails into the wood.

 a. pownd   **b.** pound   **c.** pond   **d.** puond

8. The _____ cheered when our team won the game.

 a. crowd   **b.** crowed   **c.** croud   **d.** croued

9. Who gets to take a _____ first this morning?

 a. shouwer   **b.** shour   **c.** shouer   **d.** shower

10. Liza wore a new _____ and skirt to the meeting.

 a. blouse   **b.** blows   **c.** blues   **d.** blous

**Read each hint. Fill in the blank with *ow* or *ou* to
complete the word.**

squeaks and eats cheese   m_____se

has petals and a stem   fl_____er

for drying off   t_____el

for eating and talking   m_____th

b_____nce

h_____l

Phonics • *Skills Practice*

Suffixes *-er, -or,* and *-ness*

FOCUS
- A **suffix** is added to the end of a base word. Adding a suffix changes the meaning of the word.

- The suffixes *-er* and *-or* can mean "one who." They refer to a person or thing that does a certain action.
  Examples: heat + er = heater (a thing that heats) collect + or = collector (one who collects)

- The suffix *-ness* means "the state of being."
  Example: dark + ness = darkness (the state of being dark)

PRACTICE Add the suffix *-er, -or,* or *-ness* to the base words below. Write the new word, and then write its meaning.

	New Word	**Meaning**
1. work + er =	_____	_____
2. calculate + or =	_____	_____
3. still + ness =	_____	_____
4. act + or =	_____	_____
5. goofy + ness =	_____	_____
6. manage + er =	_____	_____

APPLY Add the suffix *-er*, *-or*, or *-ness* to a word from the box. Then write the word to complete a sentence.

ill	play	sail	dancer
love	bright	illustrate	silly

7. Dr. Burns will know how to cure the _____.

8. She is the author and the _____ of the book.

9. Wear sunglasses to shield your eyes from the _____ of the sun.

10. A good _____ has rhythm and grace.

11. Children giggled at the clown's _____.

12. Did the _____ send a message from her boat?

13. Which hockey _____ scored the goal?

14. Lee is an animal _____ and has lots of pets.

Write two sentences using the words from the box.

dreamer	shyness	protector

15. _____

_____

16. _____

_____

Word Analysis • *Skills Practice*

/oo/ and /ow/

FOCUS
- The /oo/ sound is spelled *oo*.
- The /ow/ sound can be spelled *ow* or *ou_*.

PRACTICE Sort the words under the correct heading.

hook	frown	stood	pout
amount	woof	prowl	council

/oo/ spelled oo

1. _____

2. _____

3. _____

/ow/ spelled ow

4. _____

5. _____

/ow/ spelled ou_

6. _____

7. _____

8. _____

APPLY Use a word from the box to complete
each sentence.

scowl	pouch	cookies	plow	round
hoof	drown	cloud	look	flour

9. Layne keeps her pencils in a zippered _____.

10. Oranges and apples are both _____.

11. A large tractor pulls the _____ across the field.

12. There wasn't a _____ in the clear, blue sky.

13. Sally likes to drink milk with her _____.

14. The grumpy store clerk always has a _____ on his face.

15. Mix milk, butter, and _____ to make the batter.

16. The goat's _____ was covered in mud.

17. Manny likes to _____ his pancakes in syrup.

18. Never _____ directly at the sun!

Suffixes *-ly* and *-y*

FOCUS
- A **suffix** is added to the end of a base word. Adding a suffix changes the meaning of the word.
- The suffix *-ly* means "in a certain way."
- The suffix *-y* means "like" or "full of."

PRACTICE Choose a suffix from above to add to each base word. Write the meaning of the new word.

1. quick _____ Meaning: _____

2. fur _____ Meaning: _____

3. thirst _____ Meaning: _____

4. loud _____ Meaning: _____

Write three sentences using the words from above.

5. _____

_____

6. _____

_____

7. _____

_____

APPLY Add *-ly* or *-y* to the base word in parentheses ( )
to form a new word that completes the sentence.
Write the new word on the line. Then write the meaning
of the new word.

8. (Storm) _____ weather makes our pets upset.

    New Meaning: _____

9. Spread the butter (even) _____ on the toast.

    New Meaning: _____

10. A bird (sudden) _____ flew into the window.

    New Meaning: _____

11. We need to clean out our (mess) _____

    basement this weekend.

    New Meaning: _____

12. Hold the baby chick very (careful) _____.

    New Meaning: _____

13. Liza (bold) _____stepped up to the microphone.

    New Meaning: _____

14. The spilled glue left a (stick) _____ spot on

    my desk.

    New Meaning: _____

15. Trevor trimmed the dog's (shag) _____ fur.

    New Meaning: _____

Word Analysis • *Skills Practice*

/aw/ spelled *aw, au_, augh, ough, all,* and *al*

> **FOCUS** The /aw/ sound can be spelled *aw, au_, augh, ough, all,* and *al.*

PRACTICE Sort the words under the correct heading.

flaw	cause	brought	naughty	stalk	awning
recall	haunt	laundry	gnaw	false	stall

/aw/ spelled *aw*

1. _____

2. _____

3. _____

/aw/ spelled *au_*

4. _____

5. _____

6. _____

/aw/ spelled *augh*

7. _____

/aw/ spelled *ough*

8. _____

/aw/ spelled *all*

9. _____

10. _____

/aw/ spelled *al*

11. _____

12. _____

APPLY Use the letters in parentheses and an /aw/
spelling pattern to make a word.

13. (f, t)   _____

14. (k, w)   _____

15. (h, r, t, o)   _____

16. (d, e, r, t)   _____

17. (s, b, e, a, b) _____

18. (n, r, d)   _____

Circle the correct spelling for each set of words.

19. walet   wallet

20. tought   taught

21. fawlt   fault

22. calm   caulm

23. auful   awful

24. thoughtful   thaughtful

Suffixes *-able* and *-ment*

FOCUS
- A **suffix** is added to the end of a base word. Adding a suffix changes the meaning of the word.
- The suffix *-able* means "able to be or worthy of being" or "tending toward."
- The suffix *-ment* means "the act, process, or result of" or "the condition of being."

PRACTICE Add the suffix *-able* or *-ment* to the base words below. Write the new word and the meaning of the new word.

Base Word	*-able*	New Meaning
1. honor	_____	_____
2. use	_____	_____
3. remark	_____	_____

Base Word	*-ment*	New Meaning
4. pay	_____	_____
5. manage	_____	_____
6. excite	_____	_____

APPLY Add the suffix *-able* or *-ment* to a word from the box. Then write the word to complete a sentence.

agree	move	engage
advertise	depend	reason

7. We went to the store after we saw the _____.

8. Even a slight _____ causes pain in Rachel's broken leg.

9. Matt and his parents reached an _____ about his allowance.

10. Is 7:00 a _____ time for the party to start?

11. Riku is a _____ worker who shows up on time every day.

12. The happy couple announced their _____ at the party.

Write two sentences using words from the box.

lovable	valuable	judgment	treatment

13. _____

_____

14. _____

_____

Word Analysis • *Skills Practice*

/oi/ spelled *oi* and _*oy*

> ## *FOCUS* The /oi/ sound can be spelled with *oi* and _*oy.*

PRACTICE Write a letter on the line to create a word with the _*oy* spelling pattern. Then write the whole word.

1. _____oy _____

2. _____oy _____

3. _____oy _____

4. _____oy _____

Write a letter on the lines to create a word with the *oi* spelling pattern. Then write the whole word.

5. _____oi_____ _____

6. _____oi_____ _____

7. _____oi_____ _____

8. _____oi_____ _____

9. _____oi_____ _____

10. _____oi_____ _____

APPLY Write *oi* or *oy* on the line to complete each
word with the correct /oi/ spelling pattern.

11. Juan could not av_____d stepping in the puddle.

12. Lots of girls and b_____s ran around the
playground during recess.

13. P_____nt the telescope toward the stars.

14. Rain sp_____led our plans for a picnic.

15. Eliza enj_____s knitting and other crafts.

16. The cake was m_____st and tasty.

17. The r_____al family lives in a palace.

18. A tornado can destr_____ a house in seconds.

19. Please keep your v_____ces down while you are
in the library.

20. The c_____ns in Luke's pocket equal 75 cents.

21. Grace is ann_____ed by the ticking clock.

22. Our next v_____age will be a trip to Ireland.

Words with the Same Base

FOCUS A **base word** is a word that can stand alone.
A base word can give a clue to the meaning of
other words in its **word family.**
Example: base word—kind
word family—unkind, kindly,
kindness, kindest

PRACTICE Write the base word for each
word family below.

1. walks, walker, walkway

base word: _____

2. handed, handful, handy

base word: _____

3. restate, stately, statement

base word: _____

4. writer, written, writing

base word: _____

5. disfavor, favorable, favorite

base word: _____

APPLY Circle the words in the same word family.
Then write the base word on the line.

6. angles   dangled   triangle

base word: _____

7. judgment   misjudge   juggler

base word: _____

8. refund   funny   funding

base word: _____

9. generous   gently   gentlemen

base word: _____

10. hurried   unhurt   hurtful

base word: _____

11. director   predictor   indirectly

base word: _____

12. unreal   reality   leery

base word: _____

Word Analysis • *Skills Practice*

Fossils

Fossils give us clues about plants and animals that lived long ago. Scientists find most fossils buried in the ground. Have you ever seen a real fossil? Maybe you have seen a picture of a fossil. Have you ever seen a dinosaur bone? A dinosaur bone is a fossil!

There are different kinds of fossils. Some plants and animals died and were buried in mud. The mud got hard and turned into rock. Sometimes plants and animals left a print in the mud. Some of the prints were footprints. These prints turned into rocks too.

Scientists find fossils all over Earth. One of the main reasons to search for fossils is to learn more about what Earth was like long ago. Fossils provide a way to study plants and animals that are no longer alive on Earth.

Studying fossils is also a way to learn how old something is. Scientists have found fossils of the fern plant which is still alive today. That means ferns are very old!

Some of the most popular fossils are those of dinosaurs. Perhaps it is the mystery around dinosaurs that makes them so interesting. No living human has ever seen a living dinosaur. All we have are fossils.

There were lots of dinosaurs. The fossils that scientists find vary in size, but they all started off as bone. The dinosaur bones became fossils over time. Scientists collect these fossils and put them together to learn about the dinosaurs.

Sometimes the fossils are together in one place. They are the fossilized bones of the whole dinosaur. Other times the fossils are in different places. When that happens, the fossils are like pieces of a puzzle. Scientists examine each fossil. Then they put all of the fossils together for the correct dinosaur. They solve the puzzle.

So we know that fossils can come from plants as well as the bones of animals. Can you think of another kind of fossil? What about the whole body of an insect trapped inside a rock?

Some insects get stuck in the sticky liquid, or sap, that slides down the trunks of trees. Insects can get stuck in the sap. Over time, the sap gets hard. Once it becomes a solid it is called amber. Inside the amber is the body of the insect.

It is by studying the fossilized remains of animals and plants that we have any guesses about what they used to be like. Fossils are very helpful to both scientists and students. They help us learn about living things from the past.

The *ough* Spelling Pattern

FOCUS
- The *ough* spelling pattern has many different sounds.
- The letter *t* at the end of the *ough* pattern will most often cause *ough* to make the /aw/ sound.

PRACTICE Use the words in the box to answer the questions.

though	bought	dough	tough

1. Which words have the same vowel sound as *no*?

_____   _____

2. Which word has the same vowel sound as *saw*?

_____

3. Which word has the same vowel sound as *puff*?

_____

APPLY Add the given letter to the *ought spelling* pattern. Write the new word on the line.

4. s + ought = _____

5. f + ought = _____

6. b + ought = _____

7. br + ought = _____

Circle the correct word to complete each sentence.

8. Donna (bough, bought) apples at the market.

9. Do we have (enough, enought) chairs for everyone?

10. I (though, thought) class started at 8:30.

11. The children (fought, fough) over whose turn it was.

12. Use a rolling pin to flatten the cookie (dought, dough).

13. (Althought, Although) I live close to the school, I still ride the bus.

14. Raj (brought, bough) his tent for the camping trip.

15. We (sough, sought) sand and sun on our beach vacation.

Phonics • *Skills Practice*

Synonyms and Antonyms

FOCUS
- **Synonyms** are words that are similar in meaning. *Happy* and *glad* are synonyms.
- **Antonyms** are words that are opposite in meaning. *Up* and *down* are antonyms.

PRACTICE In each box, circle the *synonym* and draw a line under the *antonym* for each given word.

1. near | close | apart | far

2. winner | helper | loser | champion

3. before | beside | after | earlier

APPLY Write the synonym or antonym for the word in parentheses to complete the sentence.

4. (frown) Curtis has the warmest _____.

5. (bend) Slow down when you come to a _____ in the road.

6. (bright) Mom did not finish working until it was _____ outside, so we had a late dinner.

7. (hilarious) The _____ movie had us laughing all night long.

Multiple-Meaning Words and Homophones

> **FOCUS** **Multiple-meaning words** are spelled and pronounced the same but have different meanings.
> **Homophones** are words that are pronounced the same but have different spellings and meanings.

PRACTICE Use the multiple-meaning word and the homophones below to complete the sentences.

toad	towed	park

8. Can we _____ our car near the entrance to the _____?

9. Gina _____ the boat behind her truck.
A _____ has bumpy skin, but a frog is smooth.

APPLY Read the two meanings for a multiple-meaning word. Write the word on the line.

10. the opposite of *left* **OR** correct _____

11. a person who swings at a ball **OR** a mixture used for making cake _____

Read the two meanings for a pair of homophones. Write the homophones on the lines.

12. belonging to us_____
periods of time equal to 60 minutes _____

Word Analysis • *Skills Practice*

Silent Letters

FOCUS Silent letters in a word are not heard when the word is read.

PRACTICE Read each word. Circle the letter or letters that are silent.

1. hour

2. doubt

3. rhyming

4. scene

5. knit

6. wrench

7. lamb

8. island

9. scent

10. listen

11. crumb

12. school

13. adjust

14. knuckles

15. muscle

16. design

17. science

18. ache

19. thistle

20. autumn

APPLY Circle the correct word that completes each sentence.

21. Martin ate (hafe, **half**) of the sandwich.

22. Can you (**answer**, anser) the math question?

23. The (shent, **scent**) of roses filled the air.

24. Did you (**listen**, lissen) to the band play?

25. Cara hit her (thumn, **thumb**) with a hammer.

26. The (scine, **sign**) tells us which road to take.

Look at each pair of words with a silent-consonant spelling pattern. Underline the spelling pattern in each word. Write a third word with the same spelling pattern.

27. knee   knot   _____

28. climb   numb   _____

29. wrong   wrist   _____

30. gnat   sign   _____

31. rhombus   rhythm   _____

32. taught   daughter _____

The Prefixes *dis-*, *un-*, and *non-*

> **FOCUS** A **prefix** is added to the beginning of a word and changes the meaning of that word.
> - The prefix **dis-** means "to do the opposite of" or "not to."
> - The prefix **un-** means "the opposite of" or "not."
> - The prefix **non-** means "to do the opposite of" or "not."

PRACTICE Choose a prefix from above to add to each base word. Write the meaning of the new word.

1. _____stop _____

2. _____agree _____

3. _____planned _____

4. _____loyal _____

5. _____wind _____

6. _____fiction _____

7. _____zip _____

8. _____connect _____

APPLY Choose one of the following prefixes to add to the base word in parentheses ( ) to form a new word that completes the sentence. Write the new word on the line. Then write the meaning of the new word.

dis-	*un-*	*non-*

9. Karl was (able) _____ to attend the party.

   New Meaning: _____

10. You must speak to the principal if you (obey) _____ your teacher.

    New Meaning: _____

11. Joan (wrapped) _____ her birthday gift.

    New Meaning: _____

12. We use (toxic) _____ cleaners that are safe for the environment.

    New Meaning: _____

13. Please (connect) _____ your phone from the charger.

    New Meaning: _____

14. Toby uses (fat) _____ milk on his cereal.

    New Meaning: _____

Word Analysis • *Skills Practice*

The *ough* Spelling Pattern

> **FOCUS**
> - The *ough* spelling pattern has many different sounds.
> - Adding the letter *t* to the end of the *ough* pattern makes *ough* say the /aw/ sound.

PRACTICE Sort the words under the correct heading.

rough	though	ought

/aw/ vowel sound

1. _____

/ō/ vowel sound

2. _____

/u/ vowel sound

3. _____

APPLY Circle the correct word that completes each sentence.

4. Brad (thought, though) the party was a success.

5. Jamal was (therow, thorough) when he cleaned his room.

6. (Although, Although) Tara is young, she is very wise.

7. The bitter medicine is (tough, though) to swallow.

8. We (fawt, fought) the rapids as we paddled along the river.

Silent Letters

FOCUS Silent letters in a word are not heard when the word is read.

PRACTICE Choose a letter in parentheses ( ) to complete each word. Write the letter on the line.

9. (g, h)   desi_____n

10. (m, n)   colum_____

11. (h, k)   sc_____ool

12. (s, t)   cas_____le

13. (c, h)   s_____issors

14. (b, n)   num_____

15. (g, k)   _____nock

APPLY Unscramble the following words, and then write each new word on the line. Underline the silent letter or letters in each word.

16. t c n e s   _____

17. o b t u d   _____

18. l e w e s r t   _____

19. w e n k   _____

20. u s m l e c   _____

21. m u t a n u   _____

22. d h c r o   _____

The Prefixes *re-*, *pre-*, and *mis-*

FOCUS A **prefix** is added to the beginning of a word and changes the meaning of that word.

- The prefix **re-** means "again" or "back."

- The prefix **pre-** means "before in place, time, or order."

- The prefix **mis-** means "bad," "wrong," or "incorrectly."

PRACTICE Add a prefix to each base word. Write the new word. Then write the meaning of the new word.

1. mis + judge = _____

New Meaning: _____

2. re + play = _____

New Meaning: _____

3. mis + spell = _____

New Meaning: _____

4. pre + cook = _____

New Meaning: _____

5. re + mix = _____

New Meaning: _____

6. pre + select = _____

New Meaning: _____

APPLY Choose one of the following prefixes to add to the base word in parentheses ( ) to form a new word that completes the sentence. Write the new word on the line. Then write the meaning of the new word.

re-	pre-	mis-

7. If you (treat) _____ a car, it won't run properly.

New Meaning: _____

8. Press the backward arrow to (wind) _____ the song.

New Meaning: _____

9. Libby (cut) _____ some fabric before starting the quilt.

New Meaning: _____

10. The piano needs to be (tuned) _____ after we move to the new house.

New Meaning: _____

11. We (ordered) _____ tickets months before the show.

New Meaning: _____

12. Chris (places) _____ his phone every day, but he always finds it!

New Meaning: _____

Word Analysis • *Skills Practice*

Contrast /ōō/ with /oo/ and /ō/ with /ow/

FOCUS
- The *oo* spelling pattern can make the /ōō/ and /oo/ sounds.
- The *u, u_e, _ue,* and *_ew* spelling patterns can make the /ōō/ sound.
- The *ow* spelling pattern can make the /ō/ sound or the /ow/ sound.

PRACTICE Write the following words under the correct sound.

crowded	yellow	rookie	booth
owner	drowsy	groomer	childhood

/ōō/

1. _____

2. _____

/oo/

3. _____

4. _____

/ō/

5. _____

6. _____

/ow/

7. _____

8. _____

APPLY Unscramble the letters in parentheses ( ) to make a word with the given spelling pattern.

9. (r, c) _____ow

10. (g, d, l)_____ue_____

11. (h, s, p) _____oo_____

12. (r, f, e, l) _____ow_____

13. (l, s, a, h, l) _____ow

14. (t, t, h, r) _____u_____

Write a word for each spelling pattern listed below.

15. /ō/ spelled *ow* _____

16. /ow/ spelled *ow* _____

17. /oo/ spelled *oo* _____

18. /o͞o/ spelled *oo* _____

19. /o͞o/ spelled *u* _____

20. /o͞o/ spelled _*ue* _____

21. /o͞o/ spelled *u_e* _____

22. /o͞o/ spelled _*ew* _____

Comparatives and Superlatives

FOCUS
- The **comparative ending** -er shows a comparison between two things.
- The **superlative ending** -est shows a comparison among three or more things.
- Some words that show comparisons do not follow the usual patterns of adding -er or -est. These words are **irregular comparatives**.

PRACTICE Add -er or -est to the following words. Write each new word on the line.

1. fresh + er = _____

2. safe + est = _____

3. angry + est = _____

4. loud + er = _____

5. wet + er = _____

6. narrow + est = _____

APPLY Choose a word from the box to complete each sentence.

most	better	farther	least	worse	farthest

7. Jake hopes he sleeps _____ tonight than he did last night.

8. Five students made paper airplanes, and Rosie's flew the _____.

9. The winner is the person who scores the _____ points.

10. Buddy is a good dog and causes the _____ trouble of any pet I know.

11. The doctor said to call if my pain gets _____.

12. Is it _____ to walk to the school or the store?

Suffixes *-er, -or,* and *-ness*

> **FOCUS**
> - A **suffix** is added to the end of a base word. Adding a suffix changes the meaning of the word.
> - The suffixes **-er** and **-or** can mean "one who." It refers to a person or thing that does a certain action. **Examples:** eraser (a thing that erases) actor (one who acts)
> - The suffix **-ness** means "the state of being." **Example:** shyness (the state of being shy)

PRACTICE Add the suffix *-er, -or,* or *-ness* to the base words below. Write the new word, and then write its meaning.

13. toast + er = _____

14. sail + or = _____

15. calm + ness = _____

APPLY Add the suffix *-er, -or,* or *-ness* to a word from the box. Then write the word to complete a sentence.

fond	senate	sweep	bumpy	jog

16. A _____ is elected by the people in his or her state.

17. Marley's vivid outfits show her _____ of bright colors.

18. The _____ of the road caused me to feel sick.

19. Use a _____ to clean the floor.

20. We passed a _____ on the path in the park.

Word Analysis • *Skills Practice*

Contrast /o͞o/ with /ū/ and /aw/ with /ow/

FOCUS
- The /o͞o/ and /ū/ sounds can be spelled *u, u_e, _ue,* and *_ew.*
- The /aw/ sound can be spelled *aw* and *au_.*
- The /ow/ sound can be spelled *ow* and *ou_.*

PRACTICE Underline the /ow/ or /aw/ spelling pattern in each word. Write a rhyming word that has the same spelling pattern.

1. crown _____

2. pause _____

3. sound _____

4. claw _____

5. shower _____

6. yawn _____

Read the clue and fill in the correct /o͞o/ or /ū/ spelling pattern to complete the word.

7. a person   h _____ man

8. to say no   ref _____ s _____

9. a thick soup st _____

10. a spring flower t _____ lip

11. to disagree arg _____

12. to make dirty poll _____ t _____

APPLY Circle the correct word that completes each sentence.

13. What interesting shapes do you see in the _____?

    a. clowds   **b.** clouds   **c.** clauds   **d.** cloweds

14. Does the cost of a meal _____ a drink?

    a. inclewd   **b.** includ   **c.** inclued   **d.** include

15. Grandma's ring has great _____ to Jenny.

    a. value   **b.** valew   **c.** valu   **d.** valaue

16. A kite was _____ in the tree's branches.

    a. cought   **b.** cawght   **c.** caut   **d.** caught

17. You can count on Manny to always tell the _____.

    a. trueth   **b.** truth   **c.** truthe   **d.** trouth

18. The _____ of the storm caused a lot of damage.

    a. furye   **b.** furry   **c.** fury   **d.** furey

19. We heard wolves _____ in the distance.

    a. houl   **b.** howl   **c.** hawl   **d.** howel

20. I need to _____ this library book.

    a. renu   **b.** reknew   **c.** renue   **d.** renew

Suffixes *-ly, -y, -able, -ment* and Word Families

FOCUS
- A **suffix** is added to the end of a base word and changes the meaning of the word.

  The suffix *-ly* means "in a certain way."

  The suffix *-y* means "like" or "full of."

  The suffix *-able* means "able to be or worthy of being" or "tending toward."

  The suffix *-ment* means "the act, process, or result of" or "the condition of being."

- A **base word** is a word that can stand alone. A base word can give a clue to the meaning of other words in the **word family.**

  Example: base word—kind
  word family—unkind, kindly, kindness, kindest

PRACTICE Add the suffix *-ly, -y, -able,* or *-ment* to the base words below. Write the new word and the meaning of the new word.

Base Word	Suffix		New Word	New Meaning
1. sincere	+ ly	=	_____	_____
2. ship	+ ment	=	_____	_____
3. chew	+ able	=	_____	_____
4. ice	+ y	=	_____	_____

Write the base word for each word family below.

5. likely, unlike, likable

    base word: _____

6. unworthy, worthwhile, worthless

    base word: _____

7. investor, reinvest, investment

    base word: _____

APPLY Circle the words in the same word family.
Then write the base word on the line.

8. shaky   shacks   shakable

    base word: _____

9. easy   easily   eastern

    base word: _____

10. convertible   comforter   converter

    base word: _____

11. devalue   developer   development

    base word: _____

12. screamer   creamy   creamer

    base word: _____

13. correctly   contractor   incorrect

    base word: _____

14. manager   management   angrily

    base word: _____

Word Analysis • *Skills Practice*

The United States of America

Do you know why we celebrate the Fourth of July? It is the birthday of the United States! July 4, 1776, is the date the Founding Fathers adopted the Declaration of Independence.

Today the Unites States is a free country. But it was not so a long time ago. The United States used to be part of England. England made the laws and told people here how to live.

Many people did not like the way they were treated by England. The laws were not fair. They wanted to be free, so they decided to fight for their freedom.

People explained their reasons for starting a new country by writing the Declaration of Independence. Thomas Jefferson, Benjamin Franklin, and John Adams helped write it.

The Declaration of Independence is one of the most important writings in the history of the United States. It declared that people were free to make new rules. It talks about many of the freedoms we enjoy today. It says that all people are created equal. It also explains our rights such as "life, liberty, and the pursuit of happiness."

The leaders in the early United States of America had to make many decisions to set up their government. Some of them thought that each state should have its own government. Others believed that the states should come together to form one government. Smaller states were afraid that larger states would have too much power.

In May of 1787, the leaders of the United States met for a convention. We call this group of leaders the Founding Fathers. Many of them helped write the Declaration. They were farmers, lawyers, or traders. They all wanted to make a new set of laws that would keep the United States free.

Leaders from most states traveled to Philadelphia. Their job was to write the Constitution. The Constitution was a set of laws for the new country. It took a while to write.

In September of 1787, the Constitution was finally finished. Nine states had to approve it before it became law. This happened in June of 1788.

The Constitution explains the rights and duties of all citizens. It also tells how our government works. It set up the three branches of government, each with different powers. Each branch watches over the other two branches.

The Constitution is a living document. This means that people can make changes to it. The founders had to make some changes. Some people thought the Constitution did not protect people's rights. They wanted to add a new part to the Constitution to do this, and the founders agreed to update it.

Changes to the Constitution are called amendments. The founders added ten amendments. The first ten amendments are called the Bill of Rights.

The Declaration, the Constitution, and the Bill of Rights have granted Americans the freedoms that we have today. It is because of those freedoms that we celebrate the birth of this country on the Fourth of July.

Fluency • *Skills Practice*